PREMIERSHIP & FIRST DIVISION

FOOTBALL GROUNDS

BEFORE AND AFTER TAYLOR

Photography
by
Kevin Norminton & Chris Ambler

ACKNOWLEDGEMENTS

We wish to thank 91 of the 92 F.A. Carling Premiership and Endsleigh Football League clubs for their cooperation in the publication of both this book and the eventual publication of the one for the 2nd and 3rd Division clubs. Unfortunately our thanks are not extended to Birmingham City FC.

In addition, we are indebted to Dixons Stores Group (Grimsby Branch) for providing film and processing for the 1995 photographs.

Finally our thanks go to Kevin Norminton and Chris Ambler for providing the photographs themselves. The contributions of Ken Ferris and Mike Ross are also acknowledged.

British Library Cataloguing in Publication Data

A catalogue record for this book is available from the British Library

ISBN 0-947808-64-7

Printed by The Polar Print Group, Leicester

CONTENTS

FOREWORD

In 1990 we published a book entitled 'Full Colour Views of Football League Grounds' which was the first-ever book featuring full-colour ground photographs of all 92 Football League Grounds (photographs by Chris Ambler).

Since then the F.A. Carling Premiership has come into existence changing the face of English football dramatically. In addition, Lord Justice Taylor's Report on Football Ground Safety has highlighted the potential dangers of non-seated grounds and it is now a legal requirement for Premiership and 1st Division Football Grounds to be all-seaters.

Certain transitional exemptions to the all-seater requirement still apply to clubs planning to move to new stadia (notably Sunderland FC, Portsmouth FC and Bolton Wanderers FC) and, in addition, to clubs recently promoted from the 2nd Division.

During the Summer of 1995, Mr. Kevin Norminton undertook the mammoth task of photographing the 44 grounds of the Premiership and 1st Division clubs and, in addition has also photographed those of the 2nd and 3rd Division clubs.

We have, accordingly, used his photographs for 42 of the 44 clubs the exceptions being Birmingham City FC and Liverpool FC. In the case of Birmingham City FC, Kevin was refused admission to the stadium despite having arranged his 300-mile visit a week in advance and we are indebted to Mr. Ken Ferris who supplied the two photographs which we have used. Ken himself undertook a similar, though more arduous marathon when he attended a first-team game at every League Football Ground during the 1994/95 season! A book recounting his experiences is to be published shortly.

As regards Liverpool FC, Kevin was given permission to photograph the stadium for our other publication 'The Supporters' Guide to Premiership and Football League Clubs'. However, due to an oversight on our part, we did not seek permission to use the photographs in this book. We discovered this oversight at such a late stage that we did not feel that it would be reasonable to expect Liverpool FC to give permission retrospectively and we are indebted to Mr. Mike Ross for providing the current ground photos for Anfield.

Several clubs were playing at entirely different grounds in 1990 to the present day (Charlton Athletic FC, Huddersfield Town FC, Millwall FC, Wimbledon FC and Middlesbrough FC) and, where this is the case, we have shown comparative photographs for the grounds in use in 1990.

We are sure that you will be amazed at the developments which have taken place over such a short period of time and hope to produce the book '2nd & 3rd Division Football Grounds before and after Taylor' in the near future.

John Robinson
EDITOR

ARSENAL FC

Arsenal Stadium, Highbury - before the Taylor Report

ARSENAL FC

Arsenal Stadium, Highbury - after the Taylor Report

ASTON VILLA
Villa Park - before the Taylor Report

ASTON VILLA

Villa Park - after the Taylor Report

BARNSLEY FC
The Oakwell Ground - before the Taylor Report

BARNSLEY FC
The Oakwell Ground - after the Taylor Report

BIRMINGHAM CITY FC

St. Andrews - before the Taylor Report

BIRMINGHAM CITY FC

St. Andrews - after the Taylor Report

BLACKBURN ROVERS FC

Ewood Park - before the Taylor Report

BLACKBURN ROVERS FC

Ewood Park - after the Taylor Report

BOLTON WANDERERS

Burnden Park - before the Taylor Report

BOLTON WANDERERS

Burnden Park - after the Taylor Report

CHARLTON ATHLETIC FC
Selhurst Park - before the Taylor Report

CHARLTON ATHLETIC FC
The Valley - after the Taylor Report

CHELSEA FC
Stamford Bridge - before the Taylor Report

CHELSEA FC
Stamford Bridge - after the Taylor Report

COVENTRY CITY FC

Highfield Road Stadium - before the Taylor Report

COVENTRY CITY FC

Highfield Road Stadium - after the Taylor Report

CRYSTAL PALACE FC

Selhurst Park - before the Taylor Report

CRYSTAL PALACE FC

Selhurst Park - after the Taylor Report

DERBY COUNTY FC

The Baseball Ground - before the Taylor Report

DERBY COUNTY FC

The Baseball Ground - after the Taylor Report

EVERTON FC

Goodison Park - before the Taylor Report

EVERTON FC
Goodison Park - after the Taylor Report

GRIMSBY TOWN FC
Blundell Park - before the Taylor Report

GRIMSBY TOWN FC

Blundell Park - after the Taylor Report

HUDDERSFIELD TOWN FC

Leeds Road - before the Taylor Report

HUDDERSFIELD TOWN FC

The Alfred McAlpine Stadium - after the Taylor Report (New Stadium)

IPSWICH TOWN FC
Portman Road - before the Taylor Report

IPSWICH TOWN FC

Portman Road - after the Taylor Report

LEEDS UNITED FC

Elland Road - before the Taylor Report

LEEDS UNITED FC

Elland Road - after the Taylor Report

LEICESTER CITY FC
The City Stadium, Filbert Street - before the Taylor Report

LEICESTER CITY FC

The City Stadium, Filbert Street - after the Taylor Report

LIVERPOOL FC
Anfield - before the Taylor Report

LIVERPOOL FC

Anfield - after the Taylor Report

LUTON TOWN FC

Kenilworth Road Stadium - before the Taylor Report

LUTON TOWN FC

Kenilworth Road Stadium - after the Taylor Report

MANCHESTER CITY FC

Maine Road - before the Taylor Report

MANCHESTER CITY FC

Maine Road - after the Taylor Report

MANCHESTER UNITED FC
Old Trafford - before the Taylor Report

MANCHESTER UNITED FC

Old Trafford - after the Taylor Report

MIDDLESBROUGH FC

Ayresome Park - before the Taylor Report

MIDDLESBROUGH FC

The Cellnet Riverside Stadium - after the Taylor Report (New Stadium)

MILLWALL FC
The Den - before the Taylor Report

MILLWALL FC

The New Den - after the Taylor Report (New Stadium)

NEWCASTLE UNITED FC

St. James' Park - before the Taylor Report

NEWCASTLE UNITED FC

St. James' Park - after the Taylor Report

NORWICH CITY FC

Carrow Road - before the Taylor Report

NORWICH CITY FC

Carrow Road - after the Taylor Report

NOTTINGHAM FOREST FC

The City Ground - before the Taylor Report

NOTTINGHAM FOREST FC

The City Ground - after the Taylor Report

OLDHAM ATHLETIC FC

Boundary Park - before the Taylor Report

OLDHAM ATHLETIC FC

Boundary Park - after the Taylor Report

PORTSMOUTH FC
Fratton Park - before the Taylor Report

PORTSMOUTH FC

Fratton Park - after the Taylor Report

PORT VALE FC
Vale Park - before the Taylor Report

PORT VALE FC
Vale Park - after the Taylor Report

QUEENS PARK RANGERS FC

The Rangers Stadium - before the Taylor Report

QUEENS PARK RANGERS FC

The Rangers Stadium - after the Taylor Report

READING FC
Elm Park - before the Taylor Report

READING FC
Elm Park - after the Taylor Report

SHEFFIELD UNITED FC
Bramall Lane - before the Taylor Report

SHEFFIELD UNITED FC

Bramall Lane - after the Taylor Report

SHEFFIELD WEDNESDAY FC

Hillsborough - before the Taylor Report

SHEFFIELD WEDNESDAY FC

Hillsborough - after the Taylor Report

SOUTHAMPTON FC

The Dell - before the Taylor Report

SOUTHAMPTON FC

The Dell - after the Taylor Report

SOUTHEND UNITED FC

Roots Hall Ground - before the Taylor Report

SOUTHEND UNITED FC

Roots Hall Ground - after the Taylor Report

STOKE CITY FC

The Victoria Ground - before the Taylor Report

STOKE CITY FC

The Victoria Ground - after the Taylor Report

SUNDERLAND FC
Roker Park - before the Taylor Report

SUNDERLAND FC

Roker Park - after the Taylor Report

TOTTENHAM HOTSPUR FC

White Hart Lane - before the Taylor Report

TOTTENHAM HOTSPUR FC

White Hart Lane - after the Taylor Report

TRANMERE ROVERS FC

Prenton Park - before the Taylor Report

TRANMERE ROVERS FC
Prenton Park - after the Taylor Report

WATFORD FC

Vicarage Road Stadium - before the Taylor Report

WATFORD FC
Vicarage Road Stadium - after the Taylor Report

WEST BROMWICH ALBION FC

The Hawthorns - before the Taylor Report

WEST BROMWICH ALBION FC

The Hawthorns - after the Taylor Report

WEST HAM UNITED FC

Boleyn Ground, Upton Park - before the Taylor Report

WEST HAM UNITED FC

Boleyn Ground, Upton Park - after the Taylor Report

WIMBLEDON FC

Plough Lane - before the Taylor Report

WIMBLEDON FC
Selhurst Park - after the Taylor Report (Ground Sharing)

WOLVERHAMPTON WANDERERS FC

Molineux Ground - before the Taylor Report

WOLVERHAMPTON WANDERERS FC
Molineux Ground - after the Taylor Report

The Supporters' Guide Series

This top-selling series has been published annually since 1982 and contains : - 1994/95 Season's results and tables; Directions; Ground plans; Photos; Phone numbers; Parking information; Admission details and much more.

THE SUPPORTERS' GUIDE TO PREMIERSHIP & FOOTBALL LEAGUE CLUBS 1996

The 12th edition featuring all Premiership and Football League clubs.

THE SUPPORTERS' GUIDE TO NON-LEAGUE FOOTBALL 1996

The 4th edition, featuring all GM/Vauxhall Conference, Unibond Northern Premier, Beazer Homes Premier clubs + information on other major non-league clubs.

THE SUPPORTERS' GUIDE TO SCOTTISH FOOTBALL 1996

The 4th edition featuring all Scottish League, Highland League and East & South of Scotland League clubs.

THE SUPPORTERS' GUIDE TO WELSH FOOTBALL 1996

The 3rd edition featuring all League of Wales, Cymru Alliance and Welsh Football League clubs + Information on the 'Exiles' and other minor league clubs.

THE SUPPORTERS' GUIDE TO FOOTBALL PROGRAMMES 1996

The 1st edition featuring information on the Programmes of all 92 Premiership and Football League Clubs.

Each of the above priced £4.99 post free.

Also available : -

THE SHOOT DISABLED SUPPORTERS' GUIDE TO BRITISH FOOTBALL 1995

Priced 99p post free. Available free of charge when ordered with any of the above guides.

Order from : -

Soccer Book Publishing Ltd. (Dept. SBP)
72 St. Peter's Avenue
Cleethorpes
South Humberside
DN35 8HU

THE
25
YEAR RECORD
SERIES

Top quality 25 season histories with line-ups, results, scorers, attendances and season-by-season write-ups.

Titles currently available…

Aston Villa F.C...................... *Seasons 1970-71 to 1994-95*
Celtic F.C............................... *Seasons 1970-71 to 1994-95*
Derby County F.C................. *Seasons 1970-71 to 1994-95*
Everton F.C........................... *Seasons 1970-71 to 1994-95*
Leeds United F.C.................. *Seasons 1970-71 to 1994-95*
Liverpool F.C........................ *Seasons 1970-71 to 1994-95*
Manchester United F.C........ *Seasons 1970-71 to 1994-95*
Newcastle United F.C........... *Seasons 1970-71 to 1994-95*
Nottingham Forest F.C........ *Seasons 1970-71 to 1994-95*
Rangers F.C.......................... *Seasons 1970-71 to 1994-95*

Also available : -
Burnley F.C........................... *Seasons 1970-71 to 1994-95*

All titles are softback and priced £4.99

Available post free from : -

Soccer Book Publishing Ltd. (Dept. SBP)
72 St Peter's Avenue
Cleethorpes
South Humberside
DN35 8HU

Tel. (01472) 601893
Fax (01472) 698546

THE SOCCER BOOKSHELF

THE MAIL-ORDER SOCCER BOOK SERVICE FOR FANS THROUGHOUT THE WORLD

For details of our complete range of hundreds of books and videos including…

- **Annuals (Rothmans etc.)**
- **Club Histories**
- **Biographies**
- **Back Numbers**
- **General Soccer Titles**
- **Statistical Soccer Titles**

Write to : -

THE SOCCER BOOKSHELF (DEPT. SBP)
72 ST. PETERS AVENUE
CLEETHORPES
SOUTH HUMBERSIDE
DN35 8HU

or phone : -

(01472) 696226